PEAK DISTRICT MEMORIES

The Photographs of E. Hector Kyme

Roger Redfern

Published by Sigma Leisure - an imprint of Sigma Press, 1 South Oak Lane, Wilmslow, Cheshire SK9 6AR, England.

British Library Cataloguing in Publication Data: A CIP record for this books is available from the British Library.

ISBN: 1-85058-475-3

Typesetting and Design by: Sigma Press, Wilmslow, Cheshire

Printing and cover design by: MFP Design and Print

Cover photograph: Winter sun on Burbage Brook, Longshaw

Preface

Hector Kyme came fairly late to serious photography. A craftsman woodworker turned teacher, he was largely self-taught but he had the advantages of an eye for a good picture and the tenacity to perfect his technique. A home-made enlarger set him on the way to the production of large monochrome prints and a massive wooden tripod allowed long exposures on winter nights around his home country.

During the Second World War he was based at Dobcross, near Saddleworth but he regularly cycled the forty hilly miles over the Snake Pass to spend a weekend at home. The fact that he never owned a car perhaps helped in the quest for beauty because he never came to rely on the easy convenience that would have offered.

Through the years, he took countless young people into wild places, kindling in many of them a lifelong enthusiasm for the hills. Though he naturally had great affection for Peakland (his "homeland hills") he was very fond of Snowdonia and Lakeland. His particular favourite was the north-west of Scotland – the Hebrides and the remote hills of the far north-west. Given half a chance I think he would have packed his bags and settled in Wester Ross.

When he retired in 1971 the first thing he did was to go north to Durness, near Cape Wrath, and begin the long walk south to Dover. This he did during a very unsettled autumn, meeting people and taking photographs. The result was his book "A Million and More Strides" (Robert Hale, 1972).

Hector had another gift. Wherever he went, whoever he met, he made friends and entertained all sorts with tales and memories. He must surely have been the best-known person in his home district. This selection of his photographs from one small part of the collection will, I hope, bring pleasure to many people – for that was the main reason that Hector used a camera.

Sincere thanks go to the family of E. Hector Kyme for allowing me to select the photographs used here from their father's considerable collection of black and white prints taken during half a century of Peakland wandering.

Thanks also to Tim Farmer for invaluable assistance in the processing of the text.

Roger Redfern

Contents

Norbury

Four miles south-west of Ashbourne, overlooking the River Dove and right on Derbyshire's border with Staffordshire, this ancient settlement can be considered to be at the very fringe of the Peak District. The partly fourteenth-century parish church of Saint Mary and Saint Barlok dominates a group of buildings typifying medieval English rural life. Adjoining it is the lovely manor house, owned by the Fitzherberts from 1125 to 1881 though much of what we see today dates from 1660.

The fifteenth century tower has an unusual relationship with the rest of the church. The glory of Norbury, though, is the noble grandeur of the chancel, erected in the late fourteenth century and containing two of the finest examples of alabaster work in the country. One is the tomb of Nicholas Fitzherbert (died 1473), the other is that of his son and his wife.

On the Dove

est-known where it comes down its gorge-like limestone dale downstream of Hartington, the Dove is one of England's loveliest trout streams.

    This avian family meander under bank-side trees on a less well-known reach of the river
– where the Dove flows by Mapleton, a mile north-west of Ashbourne.

Welcome Fodder

There's a broad belt of grand pastoral countryside north-east of Ashbourne, where villages like Kniveton and Hognaston lie in the crumpled, grassy landscape. There was a severe frost on the January morning when Hector Kyme noticed this farmer feeding his flock, years before Carsington Reservoir transformed the shallow valley of the nearby Scow Brook.

Limestone Shire

In the golden age of the heavy horse the Ashbourne district saw immense breeding success in the development of the Shire. Sir James Scott Watson wrote more than forty years ago that "the sound limestone land seems to give the fullest expression to the inborn qualities that go to the making of a good Shire." The greatest of all Shire sires, the stallion "Harold", was bred close to Ashbourne. The Shire foal seen here was photographed with her dam near Windley. She maintains the high standards of the breed particularly associated with the limestone country near Ashbourne.

Cromford Swans

Cromford, a couple of miles downstream of Matlock town, is important as the earliest centre of England's once important cotton industry. Established by Richard Arkwright in 1771 the first mill was followed by others, all using the pollution-free power of falling water.

The small stream that drains the Bonsall valley, to the north-west, supplied several dams to power the mills. The big dam still enhances the centre of Cromford, the haunt of mute swans which Hector Kyme caught on film as they crossed the public highway – adults leading their half-grown offspring to some undisclosed destination.

Hilltop Fort

When John Smedley developed Matlock as a centre for therapeutic treatment in the middle of the nineteenth century he realised the value of the grim, dark stoned toy fortress he designed and built on top of Riber Hill. It would be "the ideal eye-catcher" as well as his own elevated private residence. It was not to be – his plan came to nought for lack of a reliable water supply! Instead it became a wartime food store, boys' prep school and, for the past three decades, a zoo for European fauna.

Tissington Pastorale

Pevsner described Tissington's Green "a picture of exquisite beauty" and so it is, overlooked by the Norman tower of St. Mary's and the Jacobean Hall. When this photograph was taken several decades ago the Dairy Shorthorn was still a common breed. Tissington Hall stands beyond, home of the Fitzherberts for over four centuries. The village, though, is best-known as the birthplace of Derbyshire well dressing, a relic of pagan religion when the spirits were thanked for continuing supplies of spring water. When the Black Death crossed the English countryside in the fourteenth century Tissington people escaped the scourge because of the pure water supply.

In Dovedale

It must have been grand to explore the limestone gorge where the Dove flows in the last century, when the dale-bottom path was dry and narrow and few people strayed. So popular has Dovedale become (especially within a stone's throw of the car park below the Stepping Stones) that a broad path has had to be constructed to keep the mud at bay. The route along the bottom of the dale is now little different to one through a public park.

The once open slopes with clearly visible limestone architecture have largely disappeared under a canopy of invading trees. You have to go upstream these days, near Milldale or beyond in Wolfscote Dale, to get some peace and see the dale as Johnson and Congreve knew it.

Milking Time

Hartington stands up on a little terrace a short distance east of the Dove, really capital of Dove country. Downstream the river winds through Beresford, Wolfscote and Dovedale in turn, upstream is the less well-known Pilsbury, Crowdicote and Hollinsclough territory with the brown gritstone heights above that.

Hartington used to have a market. It's still agriculturally centred but in danger of being swamped by an ever growing tide of visitors – best to avoid the place at summer weekends. Rather like Longnor, four miles to the north-west, it has the feel of a little town with an early Victorian Town Hall and picturesque cottages gathered around the Market Place and central pond.

Quite hidden away up a lane to the east and so overlooked by most visitors stands Hartington Hall, a typical Derbyshire manor house built by the Batemans in 1611. After restoration between the wars, it became a youth hostel.

Mow Cop

F ar to the west, right on the last folded hill of the south Pennines, south of Congleton, stands Mow Cop. It's a sharp little ridge rising to over 1,000 feet and gives tremendous views out across the Cheshire Plain one way and, looking to the north-east, past Bosley Cloud towards the high ground of the East Cheshire Hills beyond Macclesfield.

Not surprisingly there was a beacon tower here in the sixteenth century, replaced by the mock ruin called Mow Cop Castle in 1754. Randle Wilbraham of nearby Rode Hall put it up as an eye-catcher (possibly modelled on the authentic ruins of Castell Dinas Bran overlooking Llangollen?) and it's now a National Trust property. Mow Cop is where Primitive Methodism first saw light of day in 1807, when Hugh Bourne of Stoke held a camp meeting on the ridge. This established the movement which grew to have 100,000 members.

Western Grit

The extensive gritstone edges of Ramshaw Rocks, Hen Cloud and the Roaches look out towards the south-west near the Peak District's western fringe. These fine crags were first explored at the turn of the century by J.W. Puttrell, E.A. Baker and others. By the twenties the Roaches was established as a Rucksack Club climbing ground and in the early fifties Don Whillans led The Sloth, one of gritstone's most spectacular routes. The coarse gritstone forming these edges has weathered into the most intricate, attractive forms where scramblers can enjoy themselves for hours on end.

Winter in Wildboarclough

Taken during a long, hard winter this photograph shows Crag Hall, shooting lodge of the Earls of Derby, looking out across the clough to the 1,659 feet summit of Shutlingsloe. Undoubtedly the finest shaped of all Peakland hills Shutlingsloe is a magnificent vantage point in clear weather – out across the Cheshire Plain to the glinting Mersey and the blue promise of the Welsh hills.

The ornamental lake in the park below Crag Hall once supplied a "ladder" for James Brindley's carpet mills, each using the falling water in turn. Simple, pollution-free use of natural power.

Winter Sunbeams

A winter afternoon with more snow threatening on the soggy moor-top ridge that runs northwards from Shutlingsloe to the top-most edge of Macclesfield Forest. This backward view shows the summit cone of that shapeliest of hills from the path which has recently been realigned and provided with an artificial surface. This has rescued the moor from growing destruction from an ever widening path created by ramblers attempting to remain dry-shod on the crossing.

In the Forest

Macclesfield Forest, like the Royal Forest of the Peak, was subject to strict forest laws in the Middle Ages. It once stretched between Bosley in the south and Marple in the north. Not really a forest in the modern sense, rather scattered woodland with heathland and open, scrubby space. Its final demise as a hunting "forest" came in the late seventeenth century when Sir William Brereton developed more than two thousand acres as sheepfolds tenanted from him by sheep farmers. By 1682 the Earl of Derby had recovered his estates here and the land began a period of permanent settlement.

The snow-draped ruins of Ferriser Farm, seen here in the early seventies, may well have been one of these holdings established on former forest land in the seventeenth century. When the local water board planted solid blocks of conifers here early this century, around their new reservoirs, the old farms were abandoned; the slopes have taken on a countenance akin to that of the Middle Ages, only much denser and uniform than before.

Forest Chapel

Bleak midwinter at the delightfully situated hamlet of Forest Chapel with the Cat and Fiddle Inn in sight on the horizon (extreme left). The little church of St. Stephen is the second highest parish church in England, rebuilt in 1834 to serve the widely scattered population of hill farmers that still occupy this east Cheshire hill country. Some of the holdings have gone, buried in the sea of conifers of the twentieth century forest, or abandoned and amalgamated with neighbours.

St. Stephen's is best-known for its old rush-bearing ceremony which still takes place every August, a relic of the days when rushes were the common floor covering and new supplies were brought in from the nearby moor-edge towards summer's ending. Close by is Toot Hill, an enigmatic earthwork which may be the site of the original hunting lodge of Macclesfield Forest and may have been abandoned for the more hospitable site of Old Chamber Farm, itself demolished less than a century ago.

Spirit of the
East Cheshire Hills

There was a bitter wind blowing as we came over the watershed close to the Cat and Fiddle Inn one January morning in 1977. The head-water streams which feed the Clough Brook in Wildboarclough were almost silent under their cappings of thick ice. Shutlingsloe rises unmistakably (left) and the telecommunications tower on Sutton Common seems a lot further away than it actually is, rearing against a sky of palest blue.

Morning Shadows

$\mathbb{B}$efore the Buxton-Macclesfield turnpike was constructed the old road took a more direct line through the head of Wildboarclough by way of chilly Bottom-of-the-Oven and over the ridge to Walker Barn. As we went down on that magnificent January morning the shadows of field walls and farm buildings created wonderful designs on the crusty snow. The snowfall had here been carried on a north-east gale to plaster the foreground wall as we look west beyond Hainsclough Farm to the topmost conifers of Macclesfield Forest (top left); the old road climbs ahead to the ridge-top en route for Walker Barn.

Seventeenth-century
Speculation

All the wild hillsides west of Shining Tor, around the head-waters of the Clough Brook, which had formed part of the ancient forest lands were cleared by Sir William Brereton in the late seventeenth century. It became pioneering sheep ranch and subsequent enclosure with drystone walls has fossilised the district so that it looks much as it did three hundred years ago.

Here's a midwinter prospect to the south-west, to Shutlingsloe (left) and tower-topped Sutton Common (right) with Fieldhead Farm nearby, where the optimistic flock is close to the yard and lined-out feeding troughs.

Looking down Wildboarclough

No matter which way you look at Shutlingsloe it's an unmistakable shape. Here's a landscape looking almost due south over the trees around Bottom-of-the-Oven to the hidden trench of Wildboarclough. The sombre fingers of Macclesfield Forest cling to the snowy rim of the ridge near Forest Chapel. The sun was bright but the temperature extremely low; high clouds heralded an approaching depression – there was a heavy snowfall before the day was out.

Below Cat's Tor

The high watershed that runs southwards from Whaley Bridge includes Windgather Rocks and the 1,703 feet summit of Cat's Tor before rising another one hundred feet to Shining Tor, highest point in Cheshire.

Below Cat's Tor, to the west, is the quiet hill-and-valley terrain drained by the Todd Brook and River Dean. On the golden October day when this photograph was taken a rambling party can be seen going up the wall-side behind the forlorn shell of an empty farmhouse, a sure sign of rural depopulation in this head-water gritstone countryside.

Saltersford

In this quiet Cheshire upland it's still easy to imagine trains of ponies carrying loads of salt from the Cheshire wiches over the south Pennines to urban areas like Chesterfield, far to the east. One such saltway came over from Macclesfield, crossing the infant feeder of the Todd Brook here at Saltersford before crossing the watershed and descending into the Goyt Valley. Saltersford Hall was built in 1593, lying in the shadow of Cat's Tor, oozing still an aura of antiquity as we walk by on the way to pretty Jenkin Chapel

Near Jenkin Chapel

An old bridleway slides to the infant Todd Brook from the road junction at Jenkin Chapel before climbing steeply to the west (called Bank Lane) to Blue Boar Farm on its windy ridge-top, 1200 feet above the sea. Hidden away by the brook lies Burton Springs Farm; when Hector Kyme took this photograph on a glorious autumn morning twenty years ago the newly restored farmhouse looked out across its own pond, but during the intervening years the planted saplings have grown up to hide the dwelling from ramblers' eyes. On a day like the one shown here it's hard to imagine the record breaking cloud-burst of May, 1989 which caused untold destruction in these upland valleys between Kettleshulme and Wildboarclough.

Brink Brow

The narrow lane linking the Whaley Bridge to Macclesfield highway at sinuous Charles Head with Pott Shrigley allows this sudden view down to the south, into the head-waters of Harrop Brook. Brink Brow is the great sweep of tilted pasture that was used thirty years ago for motorcycle hill climbs. In the background is the shady profile of Billinge Hill, once the site of gritstone quarrying.

Pott Shrigley

Pott Shrigley comes as quite a surprise to a stranger approaching from the high ground to the east. A pretty lowland village, as good as any in all Cheshire. Overlooked by steep, patchwork slopes its unique name is derived from "shriggel" (a wood inhabited by shrikes) and "pott" (a pool). Pott is a local family name so this settlement may be "Pott's wood where shrikes are common." Unusually for a Cheshire church, St. Christopher's is built with millstone grit and has an especially large west tower. Nearby is mighty Shrigley Hall, seat of the Brabazon Lowthers until 1928; after which it served as a college of the Order of Silesians of St. John Bosco until 1986. It is now a luxury hotel.

White Nancy

Kerridge Hill-end dominates Bollington, that straggling town that grew suddenly after the Industrial Revolution. Served by the Macclesfield Canal and the head-waters of the River Dean and its tiny tributaries it's a busy place where massive textile mills still lurk in the background.

From Pott Shrigley and Bollington the gleaming cone of White Nancy is conspicuous on top of Kerridge. The obvious place for a beacon Kerridge Hill-end boasted a brick structure before 1810; before 1825 a Mr. Gaskell of Rainow built a round structure, painted white and called "Northern Nancy", probably after a female relative. Incidentally the leading draught horse used to haul a slab of stone to the hill-top for a seat was likewise called "Nancy". The name stuck.

The structure fell into disrepair and more recently has been sealed with a smooth coat. When Hector Kyme took this photograph on a bright autumn day in the seventies White Nancy had gathered a rash of spray paint but subsequently has been cleaned up again – a unique foreground for the broad vista towards Greater Manchester.

Adlington Hall

Out on the Cheshire Plain a couple of miles west of the nearest point of the National Park boundary Adlington Hall stands on the site of a pre-Norman hunting lodge. A tenuous corner of ancient Macclesfield Forest Adlington's wood is recorded in the Middle Ages as being sixteen miles long and three miles wide.

The Legh family have lived at Adlington for six hundred years though their home is now cared for by the National Trust. When this photograph was taken the Hall was not open and the late Mr. Legh appeared round a corner. His disapprobation verging on apoplexy sent us hastening towards the public highway!

Gale Damage, Lyme Park

From Pott Shrigley it's a walk of little more than three miles over Dale Top to Lyme Hall set in its grand park, to the north-east. A winter storm had disarmed this pond-side giant, close to where the park borders the open moor that climbs towards Dale Top and Sponds Hill. Recent estate management has improved the countenance of much of Lyme Park.

Lyme Stag

L yme was the home of the Leghs for precisely six hundred years. Red deer have adorned the park for much of that time, enclosed by the high park wall.

In the Court, Lyme Hall

The great house is Elizabethan but Leoni designed an impressive Palladian exterior early in the eighteenth century. The Kyme tripod was set up here for this study of the double flight of steps which lead up from the central court to the doors of the Great Hall. Robert Legh, third Lord Newton, presented Lyme to the National Trust in 1946, since when it has been leased by Stockport Corporation and open to the public.

Over the Crest

A cold, winter afternoon in Lyme Park and part of the red deer herd take off over the near horizon near the Cage. This amazing prospect tower, more impressive than Chatsworth's Stand, was built in 1525.

Saddleworth Gaggle

The straggling settlements that fill the floor of the Tame Valley upstream of Dukinfield include Mossley, Uppermill, Saddleworth and Diggle. This is true Pennine country; mills rub shoulders with solid, stone terraces that line the steep valley-sides below the high, gritstone moors. Hector Kyme lived and worked here during the second World War and so had a soft spot for the district. On a visit to the valley in the summer of 1975 he spent a long time getting this goose flock to pose as he wanted them, on the approach to St. Chad's church, Saddleworth.

Near Denshaw

Three miles north-west of Saddleworth various roads climb the steep slopes between stone-walled pastures to the broad crests of Pennine shoulders near the 1,000 feet contour. On days of lowering clouds, as here, there's a dreary prospect over the tops. Hector Kyme loved portraying this hard character of the north-west, especially when dramatic architectural props like these striding pylons throw out their challenge.

Above the Shelf Brook

One of the Peak District's finest valleys, the great clough drained by the Shelf Brook comes down from Bleaklow's western flanks towards the site of Glossop. It was used by the Romans to carry their road linking Melandra, lower Longdendale and Navio in the Hope Valley. This is true gritstone country, revealed here on a day of broken cloud looking to the north-east. The bold crest of James's Thorn is conspicuous on the skyline, adjacent to the rounded 2,039 feet summit of Higher Shelf Stones.

Working Collie

Mossylee is the highest farm in Shelf Brook Clough, one the largest sheep farms in the Peak District. Its team of Border collies are essential assistants, combining an almost feline creeping approach to their sheep with what was once described as "the hypnotic eye of a basilisk". They have completely replaced the old style of local sheepdogs which were of no known breed but "of great heart and unquenchable gallantry" who were "the everyday companion of moorland shepherds".

The Rocking Stone

How many aeons have passed since the lower Rocking Stone collapsed to leave its close neighbour as the most interesting tor of the group called the Crow Stones? This is part of that magnificent arm of high ground that extends northwards from Derwent Edge to eventually link up with Bleaklow, round the head-waters of the Derwent. The Crow Stones and neighbouring Outer Edge are fine belvederes in clear weather, not far to the north of 1,791 feet high Margery Hill, highest point of South Yorkshire.

Crow Stones

L iterally a stone's throw from the Rocking Stone the upstanding Crow Stones are substantial gritstone tors, plastered here on their western faces with snow driven a week earlier in a February blizzard. The entire length of these eastern escarpments, from here southwards to Baslow Edge and beyond, is decorated with tors of this type. They provide useful landmarks for the bogtrotter; interesting bouldering problems; shelter from wind and rain; grandstands to see a little further over the moor-tops.

Sometimes sombre and forbidding in low cloud, on days like the one shown they lift the spirit to the chill, cloudless sky.

Swaledale Ewe

This native of the northern Pennines has steadily spread southwards during the twentieth century so that it's now ubiquitous in highest Peakland. Selective breeding has resulted in animals with an instinct to forage and keep to open country where fertility is poor, boundary fences few or absent.

Very little supplementary feeding is practised with Swaledales, the main aim is to rear them on the hills to provide breeding sheep for lowland farms. If the dam has had reasonable grazing while suckling her usually single lamb on the high ground the latter can quite easily reach a dressed carcase weight of 28-36lbs at twenty weeks of age.

The look of a Swaledale's fleece suggests a hard texture but this is not so. It meets the high standards demanded for both carpets and rough woollen tweeds. For all these reasons the breed has largely displaced the ancient native breeds – Derbyshire Gritstone and White Faced Woodland.

Highest Bleaklow

Here on the very watershed we are at exactly 2,000 feet above the sea, midway between Bleaklow Hill and Bleaklow Stones. On a day like the one depicted the going is easy, the ground gripped by deep frost. A cloudless sky above the snow-fields gives the impression that you can see for a thousand miles. An occasional grouse call from some distant grough is all we hear. Far, white horizons beckon as we keep to the highest ground, able to cover good distances in these ideal conditions.

Blue Hare Haunt

nother superb day near the Bleaklow watershed. "A mountain hare sunning itself", Hector Kyme notes on the back of this photograph, "was more surprised than we as he leaped from near our feet. He was soon gone, over the drifts and beyond our sight." This is one of the joys of deep winter on the highest ground; the sight of the bounding blue hare in his seasonal overcoat.

Howden Moor

ate January on the highest ground between the head-waters of Derwent and Porter (or Little Don). The Kyme party saw no other people all day and the snow was very deep. Though gripped by extremely low temperatures traversing this glorious upland wasn't easy, as the photographer noted: "Hazards to fall into and scramble out of. Snow of this powdery consistency finds ways into boot tops and melts – I say, uncomfortable". But this is the best time of year up near the 2,000 feet contour: a black flash of passing grouse, a hare's tracks across the shining drifts, far views across scores of miles towards Lincoln and York. This is the sort of time we can imagine ourselves in pioneering days, likely to see a tweed-clad party striding our way led by G.H.B. Ward or Fred Heardman; ghosts from the golden age of 1900-30.

Upper Small Clough Confluence

We came down the uppermost Derwent one February afternoon after a day above Longdendale and in the last rays of the sun looked upstream from the little mouth of Lands Clough to the curve of the young Derwent where Upper Small Clough comes down below the shoulder of Fair Banks (left). On the level ground near the confluence once stood the Upper Derwent Cabin. This was an important shooting cabin , strategically placed for a large area of upper Derwent Dale and the Howden Moors. It was here that the late Tom Vernon, keeper of the Derwent Estate for fifty years, caught Fred Heardman and friends sleeping inside early one morning soon after the Great War. Coal for this cabin was kept in a hollow nearby and years later Fred met a fellow bogtrotter on Bleaklow who said he'd found lumps of coal beside the path earlier that day; he had never realized there was coal in Derwent Dale's rock strata. Fred saw the coal for himself on his way down from the tops – it was old fuel stored for the Upper Derwent Cabin more than forty years earlier and only now uncovered by erosion.

Bull Stones Cabins

The Duke of Norfolk became owner of the huge Derwent Estate in 1886, centred on Derwent Hall, long gone under the surface of Ladybower Reservoir. Many of the formerly useful shooting cabins have disappeared, no longer required in the age of Land Rover tracks or victims of wanton vandalism. The pair of Bull Stones Cabins overlooked the northern side of Broadhead Clough, adjacent to a reliable moorside spring called Lord Edward Howard's Spring these past hundred years. Beaters used the old, stone cabin at a slightly lower level, its remnants seen here on an early spring day in 1970. The guns used a substantial timber cabin that resembled a small Alpine climbing hut. The late Ray Ollerenshaw of Derwent fitted three new window frames early in the sixties but within a fortnight all fifty-two panes had been smashed! Ray Ollerenshaw finally resorted to burning "the pathetic ruins" so that vandals wouldn't be attracted up onto the higher ground – Bull Stones Cabins were clearly visible up the eastern side of Derwent Dale from Slippery Stones.

Looking to Slippery Stones

Taken a few minutes after the previous photograph we see the beaters' cabin remains and the long vista down the dale to the packhorse bridge spanning the Derwent at Slippery Stones. Much of the shadowy coniferous plantation rising in the background to Ox Hey was felled in 1994.

At Slippery Stones

Stanley Royle's fabulous painting of Derwent village, now in Sheffield City Council's collection, has the old packhorse bridge as its foreground. Known to have been repaired at a cost of £100 in 1682 it probably dates in part from the Middle Ages. It was dismantled prior to inundation by the rising surface of Ladybower Reservoir, the stones numbered and stored in a barn at the foot of Abbey Brook during World War Two. Eventually erected at the ancient ford at Slippery Stones in 1959 it is dedicated to the memory of John Derry (1854 – 1937), lover and champion of wild, open spaces and author of that well remembered classic "Across the Derbyshire Moors".

The re-erected bridge serves a useful purpose at the place on the old market road to Penistone where crossing the Derwent was always a tricky business. Hector Kyme's photograph of 1970 shows the young foreground silver birches which now block this view of the bridge and the shoulder of Little Moor Top beyond, where the snow has melted through to the heather banks.

Break in the Clouds, Bradfield Gate Head

The path from Strines, near the head of Bradfield Dale, climbs the long dip slope of Derwent Edge, to crest the ridge at Bradfield Gate Head. This is 1,675 feet above sea level, a short distance south of Back Tor. A slanting traverse north-west from the col goes down Abbey Bank to the mouth of Abbey Brook Clough. Down there, at the confluence, stood the historic Abbey Grange, outlying farm of Welbeck Abbey which had exemption from the Pope in payment of tithes of newly tilled ground in 1299. The stones of Derwent packhorse bridge were stored in a building here until re-erection in 1959. Nothing now remains of the Grange and its outbuildings – except the red tiled floor of the former dairy, surrounded each spring with banks of daffodils.

The Wheel Stones

In his 1905 classic "Highways and Byways in Derbyshire" J.B. Firth describes the "curious collections" of gritstone tors that adorn the crest of Derwent Edge southwards from Back Tor. One of these – probably the most conspicuous of all Peak District tors – is the Wheel Stones, between White Tor and the Hurkling Stones. Seen from parts of Derwent Dale or from the Moscar district to the east the Wheel Stones looks convincingly like a coach and horses crossing the moor in silhouette. As you get closer the illusion is lost – I don't think that the close-up view below gives much of an impression of a horse-drawn vehicle. It is nonetheless a fascinating grouping of millstone grit; erosion by wind, frost-and-thaw, and driving rain reveals the fairly level bedding of Kinder Scout Grit, a rougher material than the neighbouring Rivelin Grit.

Rough Weather, Derwent

The photographer is lucky to come on a comparatively rare view like this. Approaching Derwent Dam from the direction of Jubilee Cottages on a spring day in 1974 Hector Kyme took advantage of a short break in the clouds to take this shot of the overflow caught by gusts of a strong south-westerly. He compared the sound as that of "a mighty organ with full stops voicing – a joyous tumult". The fleeting sunshine lights up the background plantation in Ashton Clough and the shoulder of Nabs Wood.

Low Water, Howden

The dry summer of 1975 soon saw the level of Howden Reservoir falling to the dale-bottom. Here we are looking north-east to the mouth of Howden Clough with the bracken slopes of Bosen Holes rising above plantation level. Far away the moor-grass slopes slant to the skyline crest of Howden Edge (right) near the 1,700 feet contour. The following summer was even drier and the Howden bed dried right out; the tiny, sinuous trickle of the river assumed its pre-1912 character when this was a damless dale. The site of lovely Howden House was exposed after sixty years, where the arm of the reservoir disappears into the tributary valley (right). It had been a substantial, gritstone house standing in a wooded garden, the home of Lord Fitzalan Howard's gamekeeper.

The Great Ridge

Before reading the rest of this description, can you locate the viewpoint of this photograph? There are a couple of good clues – the far summit-topped, undulating ridge and the nearer, forest covered ridge.

Hector Kyme was standing on the rising moor not far from the head of Near Deep Clough with Lost Lad Hillend not far away to the north-east. We are looking to the south-west; the coniferous plantations cover Hagg Side (between Derwent Dale and the Woodlands Valley) and Crookstone Hill rises to the right edge of the picture. The Great Ridge dominates the background, topped by Lose Hill (left centre), Back Tor and Mam Tor. Rushup Edge continues the far horizon (right of Mam Tor).

In Jaggers' Clough

We look down this deep-set clough on Kinder Scout's easternmost flank. Anyone doing a complete circuit of Kinder Scout's plateau rim will get this view, down to the broad-topped ridge of Hope Brink which culminates in Win Hill's 1,523 feet gritstone cap (upper right). Beyond are the dark twin tops of Crook Hill (upper left) and the vague glint of Ladybower Reservoir's surface (upper centre). Dominating the middle ground is the broad top of Nether Moor, heather covered and site of a prehistoric altar. The name of this foreground clough refers to the jaggers, or men who carried loads of local produce – lead, wool, coal, – on trains of ponies across the Peak District hills. One such route came over by Edale Cross from the western lowlands, traversed out of the Vale of Edale, across Jaggers' Clough and so crossed the Roman road near Hope Cross. Then over the Ashop Valley and by Lockerbrook into upper Derwent Dale before the wild journey over Cut Gate to Penistone.

Seal Edge from Hope Woodlands

An early March day in 1974, late snow lingers on the slopes behind Upper Ashop Farm. The Roman road comes slanting down from Hope Cross, alongside the horizontal wall, to go down in front of the farm and so cross the River Ashop near the waterworks diversion dam. Along the lower part of the photograph runs the culvert that carries Ashop-Alport water down the valley before entering the tunnel that conducts it under Lockerbrook Heights to feed Derwent Reservoir.

Dean Hill is the dark shoulder above the farm and the tor-topped crest of Seal Edge swings along towards Chinese Wall and Fairbrook Naze (upper right).

Blackden Brook

O f all the many cloughs which cut up into the Kinder Scout massif that drained by the Blackden Brook is one of the best, almost assuming the scale of a Scottish glen. Not so rocky as Grindsbrook Clough or Fairbrook Clough it has grand proportions and is a wonderful way up onto Kinder's northern flank from the Hope Woodlands. Not favoured by ramblers in pre-war times when they had to run the gauntlet in the face of gamekeepers employed in part to keep trespassers off the high ground; Blackden was too exposed to view from the Snake road.

Blackden is, literally, "dark valley" on account of its deep shadowed countenance in winter – it looks north and so gets little direct sunlight between November and February.

This photograph was taken well over twenty years ago, looking from the Snake Road near Wood Houses and Blackden View Farm. Sturdy Blackden Barn stands by a meander of the chattering brook, one of the well proportioned stone barns put up in the Hope Woodlands by the Chatsworth estate early in the nineteenth century – you can still identify those remaining by their ball-topped finials on the gables. The crest of Blackden Edge stands, tor-strewn, against the threatening September clouds – all of 900 feet above the Ashop's banks (bottom).

Reverse View

An hour later the photographer's party had gained the rocks atop Blackden Edge. The clouds had blown away and they looked back the way they'd come. Blackden Barn is still in the picture (left centre) and beyond the re-aligned Snake Road (this section had always been subject to subsidence and the barn at Wood Houses collapsed decades ago) Blackden View Farm stands beside its sheltering copse. Slanting across the top of the photograph is the line of the Melandra to Navio Roman road, and the drainage grooves under Hey Ridge beyond it.

Alport Mouth

hereas the previous photograph was taken with a telephoto lens, bringing background detail seemingly close to the observer, this one was taken minutes later (from a nearby viewpoint) with a standard lens. Blackden View Farm is still clearly visible but now our belvedere opens up the prospect of lower Alport Dale. Almost directly above the farm is Alport Castles, Britains largest landslip. Ranged across the far horizon is the lofty watershed extending from Outer Edge to the declivities of Abbey Brook.

Wood Moor Cabin

A steep pony track winds up from the River Ashop near the Fair Brook confluence. It is seen clearly from the Snake Road near Upper House Farm and at the top, where the track crosses into Gate Side Clough, the Wood Moor Cabin was glimpsed. It was a strong timber cabin, with a timber inner lining and served shooting parties and ramblers for many years. There was no better place to sit for a while, out of the wind, and look across the valley to Bleaklow's far skyline. Suddenly, about 1960, it was vandalised – furniture and windows smashed, the lining ripped out and burnt. The weather got in, it collapsed. Hector Kyme's photograph of the late sixties shows the last days of one of the Peak District's best situated shooting cabins, with the conifers of Cowberry Tor behind. The distant crest below the breezy, March sky (left) is Higher Shelf Stones, at 2,039 feet the eighth highest Peak District summit.

In Ashop Clough

When an attempt was made to close the ancient right of way between Hayfield and the Snake Inn by way of Ashop Clough (the famous Snake Path) a group of outdoor enthusiasts fought the plan. They set up the Peak District and Northern Counties Footpath Society and won their case. That was in 1894 and the Society has continued ever since to fight for the maintenance of rights of way in the district.

This very useful bridge over the River Ashop links the Ashop Clough path (high up to the right) with Black Ashop Moor below Kinder Scout's northern Edge. The Ashop Clough Cabin stood at the top of the short flight of steps seen here. Being so close to a public path it received the unwelcome attention of vandals soon after World War Two. Keeper Joe Townsend recalled catching two men chopping up the cabin door for firewood. They appeared at the magistrates' court and were fined heavily. The building has now gone but its foundations are easy to find.

On Black Ashop Moor

There are lots of crashed aircraft remains high in the Dark Peak, their stories have been well documented. Hector Kyme and I became separated on the drab tussock slopes below Kinder's Edge one winter afternoon. He tried to make contact with finger whistling (he was skilled at this) but the high wind rendered it useless. Just having decided to head down to the river and "there to signal at intervals with a large handkerchief" he came on these aircraft remains and soon afterwards espied me lurking in the ruins of Black Ashop Cabin.

This is a wing of one of a pair of Sabres of 66 Squadron which disappeared mysteriously in July, 1954. It seems that the two planes had touched in flight and come down not far from the Snake Path, killing both pilots.

Black Ashop Cabin

This is the cabin Hector Kyme saw across the moor, where I was waiting for him on that winter afternoon (previous photograph). The Victorian cabin stands at 1,800 feet, directly below the 2,049 feet spot height on The Edge. It was located here because of the adjacent spring. Derelict since the twenties Fred Heardman recounted how a friend who should have known better indulged in stone-rolling from the crest of the escarpment above. One of his toppled boulders scored a direct hit and crashed through the cabin roof. It was the beginning of the end! Note in this photograph the stone inscribed by ramblers over fifty years ago.

Along The Edge

art of Kinder Scout's northern escarpment – The Edge – has some of the finest gritstone architecture of the Dark Peak. It was a breezy spring day when this photograph was taken, not far west of Fairbrook Naze.

Half a mile away can be seen the dark profile of the famous Boxing Gloves, a group of tors first made famous in the camera studies of the late Walt Poucher. To the right is the broad and peaty hollow of uppermost Ashop Clough, with Ashop Head rising to the gentle dome of Mill Hill (1,761 feet) beyond. Far away, over the Ashop Head horizon, can be made out the faint profile of Coombes Edge (upper right).

Westward Prospect

Crossing the northern part of Kinder Scout's plateau-top brings us to the line of escarpments facing west, out over the great space draining to the River Sett. This late spring view takes in William Clough and the gentle profile of Leygatehead Moor. Far away on the skyline stands the unmistakable outline of Coombes Edge (compare with the far background of the previous photograph). This is the setting for Mrs Humphry Ward's novel "The History of David Grieve". The story starts here on the western flanks of Kinder Scout in the middle of the nineteenth century. Anyone intimate with this side of Peakland will relish her descriptions of "magnificent curving front of moor", "grey and scattered farms which climb the long backs of moorland", and "the green swell just below whereon stood Reuben Grieve's farm, to the far-distant Alderley Edge".

Above The Downfall

A January sundown at the place where the Kinder River leaves its birthplace plateau. The day-long mist has just blown away to show a patch of blue sky and cloudlets picking up a few, pale sunset tints. The name Downfall seems to first appear on an Enclosure Award of 1840. The lone figure looks out to the south-west, over the mist-shrouded ridges that fall from left to right, culminating in the far profile of Chinley Churn that slips towards Hayfield and Birch Vale in the Sett Valley.

Over The Edge

Old snow has compacted to form ice as we look down to the crest of the Downfall, where the Kinder River drops from the high plateau. The year is 1969 – exactly fifty years after my father took a similar photograph. That was in the days when you ran the risk of arrest for trespass or took the trouble to obtain written permission. Three years later – on 13th October, 1922 – my father and a friend were seen near the Downfall; it was the height of the grouse shooting season. Their names were taken by the keeper and, a few days later, the landowner's solicitors wrote to my father demanding an apology and 6/8d (33.5p) for their fees. Failure to comply would result in court proceedings. Wisely, my father complied and thereafter obtained a written permit when venturing onto any part of Kinder Scout.

The Downfall is at its most spectacular when a south-westerly gale blows back the stream to form a plume seen from far away across the Cheshire Plain. It's also dramatic when gripped by frost, forming great vertical columns of ice.

In The Cloughs

The hand-shaped system of streams which drain Edale Head (the upper end of the Vale of Edale) come together below Jacob's Ladder, an area called The Cloughs. The Kyme party here seen going down beside the infant River Noe make a foreground for this textbook view of interlocking spurs. The sun shines on the snow-seamed northern flanks of Lord's Seat and the complex landslip terrain of Mam Tor where the Mam Nick road twists up towards the skyline (upper left).

Youthful Noe

The main feeder of the young Noe in the steep, spur country of The Cloughs. The last snow of a long winter lurks here on an Easter day, a memorial to the death of a young rambler who died nearby from hypothermia in January, 1978. Up to the left is the well-known Jacob's Ladder, named in honour of the resident of Edale Head House – Jacob Marshall – who used packhorses to carry local wool to Stockport. He constructed the steep path up towards Edale Cross to shorten the outward journey and it's been known as his Ladder ever since.

Youngit Bridge

This pretty, strategic packhorse bridge spans the infant Noe at the foot of Edale Head, where Jacob's Ladder swings up to tackle the first rise towards Edale Cross. The foreground stones in the photograph reveal the rotten, weathered state of the old track until a few years ago. The lower section of it has now been beautifully reinstated, using the ancient method of end-on stone, so that the surface looks totally in keeping with its surroundings.

Brian Redhead thought the restored track looked "as though it hadn't been touched by the hand of a man for a couple of centuries" – true praise for sensitive restoration. The shallow trench leading off to the right is the old, dog-leg lane that goes up to Edale Head House, now but a heap of stones. It was the highest, and last, dwelling in the district which John Derry aptly described as "lying darkly" on the slope towards Edale Cross. Youngit Hollow lies adjacent so this house (at 1,260 feet) was often called Youngit House. It had the date 1768 carved on it, together with the initials of John and Mathew Cooper and the Jacob Marshall who gave his name to the steep path nearby. The last resident, called Brown, departed about 1894, no doubt unable to put up with the hard life any longer. The place was left to the tender mercies of the elements; when I first knew Youngit House it was a substantial building and it wasn't a surprise to learn the place was haunted.

Heading for High Ground

Hector Kyme's daughter and a friend follow the good dog "Robbie" on a bright March morning. Once across Youngit Bridge they will climb by Jacob's Ladder to Edale Cross. From that 1,825 feet col the open country of Kinder Scout lies to the north, Brown Knoll and Colborne ridge to the south – the choice is theirs.

On Grindslow Knoll

Little more than a mile east of Edale Head, along the southern rim of the Kinder Scout plateau beyond Whipsnade and Crowden Tower, the best-known and one of the most dramatic Peak District cloughs cuts north-westwards. It is Grindsbrook Clough, which makes the most interesting approach to the plateau from this side.

Hector Kyme came across the frozen drifts from Crowden Tower and saw this prospect towards the east thirty years ago. Several weeks of low temperatures had locked ramblers' footprints on the nearby snow-field, rising past the Mushroom towards the summit of Grindslow Knoll (extreme right). Blocking the lower part of Grindsbrook Clough (left) belts of old snow stripe the side of The Nab, below Ringing Roger, and Lose Hill and, faintly, Win Hill lurk in the frosty haze.

Upper Grindsbrook – February

It takes great skill to produce a composition like this, so that part of the Peak District assumes the character of the Scottish hills, even the Alps. Hector Kyme positioned himself overlooking the western crest of the uppermost section of Grindsbrook. There he waited a long time for a climbing party to come into sight and, luckily, take a good line up onto the opposite crest. Grindslow Knoll dominates the entire landscape.

Upper Grindsbrook–
June

Compare this with the previous photograph. It's a bright day in early summer and the photographer has moved his position across the Grindsbrook ravine (to somewhere near the prominent cornice in the earlier picture). His dog and friend sit atop the bold tor which dominates this part of the upper valley.

Summer Trickle

In dry, summer weather the Grinds Brook is reduced to a friendly rill so that the ascent of the upper clough is best done up the bed of the ravine. The scramble from ledge to ledge allows rapid progress to the plateau's rim not far from the site of the former Four Jacks shooting cabin. At 1,965 feet it was the highest cabin in the Peak District, destroyed by vandals years ago, its final remnants cleared away so that a stranger could now easily miss this historic site beside the sandy meanders of the stream which was already "Grymesbroke" by 1342.

The Hope Valley

Gateway To The Hills

Hector Kyme introduced countless young people to open country. Here's a miserable sort of day in 1967 as his party of pupils from Sheffield's Newfield School alight from a Manchester bound stopping train at Edale. A note on the reverse of this particular print highlights his ever optimistic spirit: "Awful weather (no such thing). Use sound judgement as to freakish storms – snow, wind, frost, fog – and be able to bring everyone back safely. Otherwise don't go! If necessary keep to the lower ground – plenty to see there, too. If you go high have a sensible approach – compass, map, food, good clothing – then it's a challenge."

He never lost anyone on the hills. And when he took this photograph he couldn't have realised how soon it would assume the character of a period piece. The locomotive is a Midland Region Class 2 2-6-0 with Ivatt taper boiler, a class first introduced in 1946 for hauling stopping passenger trains. Steam traction on British railways came to an end in the year after this photograph was taken, in August, 1968.

Overstones and Stanage South

The most popular gritstone climbing edge of the Peak District is definitely the long escarpment of Stanage Edge, stretching from Stanage End near Moscar in the north to the Black Hawk area near the Cowper Stone in the south. A bleak March afternoon in 1975 shows new snowfall highlighting the in-bye land surrounding Overstones Farm. Standing at 1,250 feet above sea level this ancient holding was for a long period the home of the famous farming family of Priestley.

Mrs Priestley struggled here in Victorian times to bring up her six sons single-handed. Some of her descendants became outstanding shepherds and sheepdog trialists. The name Priestley remains synonymous with sheep and sheepdogs in the Hope Valley.

Callow Farm and Higger Tor

A bitter east wind was blowing down the dale-head towards the photographer on this March morning in 1975. From this angle, on the narrow road that comes up The Dale from Hathersage towards Overstones and Upper Burbage Bridge, Higger Tor presents its least well-known, western face to us. Heavy clouds cover the sky as Friesian heifers forage in the old snow, let out of their shed for exercise and fresh air. Hector Kyme recounted the trouble he had getting the left-hand animal into a satisfactory position for this composition, even then he wasn't very happy with this "tail-end vista." A moment later, though, she was in a far worse position – completely hiding the middle pair of heifers.

Callow Farm lies beside the rough track below Higger Tor. In this small homestead one of Mrs. Priestley's sons, Peter, wrestled a living from the unco-operative hillsides to support his own family. It had a sad ending. He supplemented his earnings by taking in and training other farmers' sheepdog puppies and early in 1923 he had a pair of young dogs in hand. While his own dog "Jed" went off across the moor to fetch some sheep he stood with the trainees near the highway, not far from the Fox House Inn. The young dogs wandered into the path of an approaching lorry; Peter dashed into the road and saved the dogs but was run-over himself. He was taken to hospital and died a week later; faithful "Jed" brought the sheep to the roadside gate and held them there for three hours, unaware that his master was not going to return. Peter Priestley's son found "Jed" still on duty later that day and took him home.

Callow Farm stands now a forlorn ruin on its hillside. Ivy clothes its walls, upland winds sigh through a few sentinel trees.

Spirit of the Hills

The Border Collie has completely replaced the old English sheepdog generally used up to the beginning of the twentieth century in this part of England. Peak District sheepdogs of long ago were "sturdy, of no known breed but of great heart and unquenchable gallantry".

Hector Kyme loved the challenge of animal portraiture and this one shows a modern Border Collie of the sort seen right across our hills – "fast as the wind and supremely intelligent."

Under Stanage Edge

A light covering of snow picks out fallen blocks at the foot of Stanage. It also highlights millstones fashioned here in the last century and abandoned when the market for them suddenly collapsed.

Men and teams of horses once carted great numbers of millstones down the dip slope of long moors by Redmires and Ringinglow to Sheffield and the lowlands beyond. They were used primarily in corn mills and for putting an edge on the city's "edge" tools

Beyond Overstones

A flash of passing sunlight picks out Overstones Farm from the place where the road curves over the southernmost end of Stanage, towards Upper Burbage Bridge. A fierce gale was blowing on the November day in 1971 when this photograph was taken. "Despite the 1/500 second shutter speed", Hector Kyme wrote, "I couldn't hold the camera still enough and slight "movement" is visible on the print". In the middle distance is the unmistakable shape of the coniferous plantation near Dennis Knoll, the broad, rolling back of Bamford moorland which rises to the crest of Bamford Edge and, further off (left), the conical summit of Win Hill. Vaguely beyond that is easternmost Kinder Scout; the sharp crest of Crookstone Knoll looks scores of miles away in this light (top centre).

A Sunny Corner, Stanage

Generations of photographers have delighted in the patterns of light and shade that old millstones create under several Peak District edges. This group, shown on a June evening, lie at the foot of Stanage Edge near its southern end. Impressive collections of millstones decorate the silver birch woods at Lawrence Field, not far from the Surprise View, and beside the level track between Upper Padley and Greenwood Farm.

Hood Brook Dale from Stanage

One of the joys of long summer evenings is the chance to reach the crags and see views like this. The photographer loved late light across the fairy woods that hang on the slopes of Hood Brook Dale and this picture goes some way to explain his enthusiasm.

Here we are upon Stanage Edge, south of Stanage Plantation, looking to the south-west. North Lees Hall stands in the small group of bright, deciduous trees close to the centre of the photograph. The shadowy wood on Ridgeway Side leads the eye towards the Derwent Valley and Offerton (top left). This is Brontë country – for it was here that Charlotte set much of the background for "Jane Eyre" It isn't hard to understand the spell this landscape cast on her imagination when staying with her friend, Ellen Nussey, at Hathersage vicarage in 1845.

Homeward Bound

A class 25 Sulzer-engined locomotive draws a stopping train into Hope Station about 1965. After a day on the hills the school party is ready for the ride home and prospect of a large tea. The unmistakable profile of Lose Hill is unchanged; Hope Station's booking office and waiting room is but a memory.

Hazelford Hall

This is one of the famous seven halls of the Hathersage district connected with the ancient family of Eyre. The story goes that Robert Eyre was one of the family that originated at Hope in medieval times and it's supposed that he was living at Highlow Hall, between Hathersage and Abney, when he built a Hall for each of his seven sons, each one in sight of the others. They are Offerton, Upper Shatton, Nether Shatton, Crookhill, North Lees, Moorseats and Hazelford.

On the snowy day when this photograph was taken from Abney Lane, above Leadmill Bridge near Hathersage, Hazelford is conspicuous below the tree-rimmed shoulder that leads to Eyam Moor and the 1,407 feet top of Sir William Hill.

Beyond Grindleford Station

The Midland Railway Company built its Sheffield-Manchester route through the Hope and Edale valleys as one of the last major rail links in the country. Hector Kyme's grandfather helped excavate the 3 miles 950 yards of Totley Tunnel, linking the Sheaf and Derwent valleys, between 1888 and 1893. This photograph shows preserved Stanier Class 5XP "Jubilee" No. 5586 "Bahamas" hauling a special train at speed. It is passing Grindleford sidings *en route* for Hathersage on 17th June, 1973, behind it the steep hill pastures near Leam Hall look surprisingly close through the telephoto lens.

The arrival of this line brought the Hope Valley within commuting distance of Sheffield after 1894 and resulted in the development of lots of substantial houses in Nether Padley, Grindleford, Hathersage and Bamford.

The nostalgic aroma of smoke from occasional passing preserved locomotives like "Bahamas" brings back memories to those who travelled daily by train to work in Sheffield or Manchester; and to those whose seaside holidays began with a train ride through the Hope Valley.

Surprise View

One of the best-known viewpoints in the National Park is the Surprise View, where the A625 highway from Sheffield cuts through the extreme southern end of Millstone Edge and turns northwards down the scarp slope towards Hathersage Booths. In clear weather there's a picturesque prospect up the length of the Hope Valley, framed by the encircling hills. But if you turn slightly to the left (west) a different balance of hill and dale is seen. Hector Kyme had a good eye for the slightly unexpected view and this photograph proves the point.

We are looking beyond the foreground silver birches of Greenwood Farm land, National Trust owned, across the unseen meanderings of the Derwent to the patchwork of plantations overlooking the mouth of Bretton Clough (left). Callow Farm (different to the previously mentioned one) lies high on its slope (immediately right of the small, central silver birch). Above rises the bold mass of Offerton Moor and on the far horizon (left of centre) the crests of Bleak Knoll and Bradwell Edge. Here is as fine a landscape for a mixed ramble as any you'll find – riverside, steep woodland, hill pastures and open heather moor.

Winter Sunlight at Abney

As unspoilt as any village in Peakland Abney stands at 1,000 feet overlooking the northern flank of Abney Clough, a tributary of Bretton Clough. It is the major settlement of the mass of gritstone country which makes an incursion into the limestone that dominates the central Peak District.

At the Domesday Survey the little settlement was "Habenai" – "Abba's well watered land" on account of the several springs which rise on the moor immediately above the village. It is easy to realise that this was, not long ago, a collection of working farms. There are still farms here but somewhat diluted by cottage conversions.

In this Kyme photograph, dated to the seventies by the milk churns awaiting collection, we have our back to the Derwent Valley and look towards Camphill and Great Hucklow. The foreground footpath sign points to Stoke Ford at the confluence of Abney Clough with Bretton Clough.

New Year's Day, Longshaw

The Duke of Rutland disposed of his Longshaw Lodge in 1927. There was the shooting lodge, gardens, park and farms, and grouse moors; a total of 11,533 acres. There was a real danger that parts of the estate would be sold for building houses but good fortune smiled on Longshaw at that critical time. Sheffield and Chesterfield councils decided to buy most of the high moorland for water gathering so that became secure from the shadow of commercial development. The buildings and remaining 747 acres were saved when a joint committee was set up involving Sheffield City Council and the Sheffield Association for the Protection of Local Scenery (precursor of the local CPRE branch) using a £13,000 bank overdraft. By 1931 the conveyance of the estate to the National Trust had been completed.

Since that time people have been free to roam the Longshaw estate but on the New Year's Day when Hector Kyme took this photograph he was the only human around despite the bright sunshine.

The Coldest Day

This photograph and the two following were taken on what the photographer described as "the coldest day of my experience". Here is the Burbage Brook at the foot of Longshaw Meadows, trickling between ice-crusted boulders a little upstream of the nick point where it enters the wood-girt Padley Gorge for the headlong chase towards the Derwent Valley below Nether Padley.

Frugal Fare, Longshaw

"The sun came out briefly as I walked uphill from Burbage Brook", is Hector Kyme's comment on the reverse of this photograph. The snow had lain a foot or so deep for several weeks; the ewes resorted to rummaging in search of meagre forage. "It was a good day for photography", Hector wrote, "but the shutter was in danger of freezing in these conditions".

Bleak Burbage

Down beside the icy brook again Hector took this photograph as the light began to fade and a freezing fog developed. He entitled it "The Bitter Cold" and notes on the reverse side that "for four hours I saw no-one and then turned back towards the city". His walk involved a traverse of Longshaw Meadows and along the main road by Fox House Inn and down by Strawberry Lee to Dore, to catch a train for home.

Waiting for the Signal

The first sheepdog trail at Longshaw was staged on a March day of strong winds and driving rain in 1898. It took place in the Wooden Pole Field, a most exposed spot near the junction of the Froggatt Edge and Owler Bar roads. So bad was the weather that the event was eventually stopped and tried again the next day on the more sheltered Timothy Field, near Longshaw Lodge. That was a great success and a second trial took place in September of the same year. Ever since then the annual trails have taken place each September on Longshaw Meadows.

Hector Kyme used a 200mm telephoto lens to get this close-up of a pen of Welsh Half-bred ewes, gathered ready for the next contestant to take round the course.

A Tricky Moment

In the upper picture, things are in the balance as a trio of Welsh Half-breds show defiance and test the nerve and eye of competitor and his Border Collie in Longshaw Meadows. Will the leading ewe make a run for it and upset the final outcome? No, it seems that the Welsh spirit has waned in the face of what has previously been described as "the hypnotic eye of a basilisk". That wicked gaze allied to an almost feline creeping approach make the Border Collie the supreme sheepdog.

Spring Brook

The birch and oak wood which clings to the sides of Padley Gorge, cut by the Burbage Brook downstream of Longshaw Meadows, is a rare survival of the true relict woods which once grew over a good proportion of the gritstone moors.

Here is that brook in the gorge some distance above Upper Padley. The secret of photographing falling water successfully is to use a shutter speed sufficiently slow to reproduce the impression of movement without unsatisfactory blurring of the image; this picture shows how it should be done.

On Ramsley Moor

Some older readers will remember the low profile of Ramsley Lodge upon the crest of Ramsley Moor, just east of the Sheffield to Baslow high road (see page 113). Its last occupant was Ritchie Bramwell, here seen setting out for work on the Eastern Moors. Far away (left) is the profile of Birchen Edge, topped by the Three Battleships (extreme left), gritstone tors carved with the names of three of Nelson's men o' war.

The photographer has caught the moment particularly well; we sense the gusting wind and the speed of the leading dog is emphasised by a shutter speed that tousles its legs. The camera's position makes the best of the windy, cloudy sky above the broad backbone of Calton Pastures.

A native of Edale, Ritchie was a craftsman – shepherd, as much a part of the moors as was his flock. This photograph was taken from near the door of his moor-top home, from where the Bramwells looked out to the wind-bent birches and, in early summer, heard the calls of cuckoo and wheatear. Ritchie has long gone, Ramsley Lodge but a memory; a few stones mark the graves of his beloved Collie-workmates.

Above Baslow

Anyone crossing by the footpath by Gregory Field, below the face of Gardom's Edge, will cross the Sheffield – Baslow high road near Cupola Cottage and cross the burbling Bar Brook by a delightful stone bridge, quite hidden in the tall trees from the public gaze. The path climbs the boulder strewn scrubland towards the west, steeply up to the end of Baslow Edge and conspicuous Wellington's Monument. Sometimes you will be lucky to discover in that tilting, boulder-strewn wood this herd of Highland cattle. It took several visits before Hector Kyme managed to get some of the animals in open ground and positioned satisfactorily.

Old and New Edensor

W hen the sixth Duke of Devonshire had Edensor moved from its ridge-top site in 1839 Joseph Paxton, his landscape consultant, planned the new village on the sloping ground to the west, out of sight of his employer's windows. Fallow deer are crossing the gentle ridge where old Edensor stood, crossing below a Sweet Chestnut in the limpid sunlight of a January day in 1978. Some of John Robertson's village dwellings and Sir George Gilbert Scott's church of St. Peter (1867) lie beyond.

Rich Pickings

After being released from London Zoo and a few other places in this country the Grey Squirrel has become ubiquitous, filling the niche left by the native Red Squirrel after that species had been decimated by disease. Most Greys are confident, outgoing characters and when used to close encounters with humans are fairly easy subjects to capture on film.

Hector Kyme spent a long time and a bagful of nuts, though, before he managed this portrait in Chatsworth Park.

Waiting for Spring

Chatsworth Park has two herds of deer. The pretty Fallow Deer are normally seen as pale, far off groups easily mistaken at first for sheep. The Red Deer, on the other hand, is "the largest and noblest surviving member of the ancient British fauna". Most sightings in England these days will be the "semi-domesticated" herds enclosed in large parks.

"There was a fierce frost and no sun when I saw this group of red deer under isolated trees", notes the photographer on the reverse of this print. "It was 1st February , 1972 and the light was poor so that I was obliged to use the slow speed of 1/60 second at f3.5 using FP4 film".

The snow has allowed the creation of an arresting picture, without the white drapery the deer would not be conspicuous and the tree branches wouldn't be highlighted.

Silent Winter

Snow used to excite Hector Kyme. "It brings the world alive", he used to explain, "it makes the everyday a little magical". He poked about on a bitterly cold winter day about 1970 to find the viewpoint for this photograph immediately west of Edensor.

Sir George Gilbert Scott's St. Peter's is dusted, like the rest of the village, with new snow. The spire points to leaden clouds seemingly full of snow. A silent day when no-one is about.

Guide Post, Handley Lane

The Peak District, in common with the North York Moors, has many old direction stones. Some are medieval like Wibbersley Cross on Leash Fen and Godfrey's Cross on Ramsley Moor (see page 113), others date from the great turnpike and enclosure age, like the one at Bleak House, Eastmoor.

A low-angled winter sun highlights the inscription on this direction stone at the ridge-top junction a mile west of Edensor village. Handley Lane is the way towards Pilsley and Baslow, beyond which the Bar Road took the traveller up onto Baslow Edge-end before the traverse of Ramsley Moor en route for Sheffield. Edensor Lane leads to the Derwent crossing and the steep climb onto Eastmoor before the long descent to Chesterfield.

In Haddon Tunnel

On 25th May, 1860 the Midland Railway Company gave authority for the line to be extended beyond Rowsley, for 15 miles to Buxton, involving a rise of 675 feet. The Duke of Devonshire refused permission for the line to pass through Chatsworth Park but the Duke of Rutland agreed, providing the railway was hidden for its entire passage through his Haddon Hall Park, just behind the house.

The line was excavated from the hillside, partly by cutting and partly by tunnelling. The cutting was then arched over with masonry and filled in with rock and soil to form the 1,058 yards long Haddon Tunnel. The through line was opened to passenger traffic in 1867 and closed in July, 1968. This photograph was taken soon afterwards, at the time when the tracks were being removed.

The Wye in Flood

The "Badecan weillon" mentioned in AD 924 had become "Badequella" at the Domesday Survey and "Bakewalle" by 1351. The name originates from "Badeca's spring", obviously a reliable water supply which gave rise to this settlement on the slope above the River Wye. Taken at sundown on a February day in 1965 the Wye has again overflowed its banks. Rising into the sunset sky is the spire of All Saints church. The spire was taken down in 1826 and for two decades that landmark was missing while the upper parts of the tower (dating from about 1340) where rebuilt.

The town saw a bit of unrest in 1796, when folk from surrounding villages got it into their heads that Derbyshire was required to raise more men for service in the Militia or pay a bigger quota than adjacent counties. A mob marched on the town one market day, armed with clubs and spades. After speeches in front of the Town Hall they vowed to return when the magistrates were sitting. This they did, the crowd swelled by people from as far off as Castleton and Eyam. They burst into the room where the magistrates were gathered, snatched various documents and set fire to them ceremoniously outside the White Horse Inn. This was too much for the magistrates and for their own protection they applied for a squadron of cavalry to be present at their next meeting. The mob duly appeared a third time and the mounted troops took six prisoners. These ended up in Chesterfield gaol. That seems to have been enough for the local protesters for their activities quickly died away. The long term effect of the excitement, though, was that the Epiphany Quarter Sessions were moved from Bakewell to the security of Derby!

Cooling their Heels, Bradford Dale

One of the White Peak's loveliest little rivers is the Bradford – literally "the broad ford", presumably the crossing directly to the south of Youlgreave – which rises near Elton and curves in its deep, limestone dale below Middleton and Youlgreave before joining the Lathkill at Alport. J.B. Firth considered Bradford Dale "for peaceful loveliness and sheer prettiness no thing in Derbyshire excels it". That was written in 1905 and nothing has changed much since. Hector Kyme took this photograph looking upstream exactly seventy years later, on the occasion of the centenary of Youlgreave's annual well dressings.

"No Flies on Me!"

This pedigree Shorthorn bull was resting in a pasture on Middleton Common on a July day, not far from Arbor Low, the Peak District's premier prehistoric monument. In those days the Shorthorn was still a common sight in these parts, today you will go a long way before finding any. A 200mm lens and tripod were used.

White Peak Industry

The National Park boundary makes a long detour to avoid the great limestone quarries south-west of Buxton. The bleak upland has been worked for centuries but only on a massive scale since Victorian times. This photograph, taken at sunset during 1969, shows Hindlow Quarry and the sort of affront to the landscape such quarrying and associated lime burning causes.

Above Cave Dale

Castleton stands right on the edge of surface limestone, where it shows some abrupt walls along the southern margin of the Hope Valley and is overlain by newer shales and shale grits to the north.

Cave Dale's very narrow mouth lies right at the edge of Castleton village. You turn a corner and there is the rock-girt entrance to this impressive dry valley. Hector Kyme climbed high up the side of Cave Dale on a bright summer day thirty years ago to obtain this view of Peveril Castle perched on its crag overlooking the dale. Far away the millstone grit-capped Great Ridge makes a bold skyline, including Back Tor and Lose Hill (right).

Peveril Castle has been described as the "finest medieval landmark of the Peak District". Built by the Normans and enlarged by Henry II in 1176 the castle seems to have lost its importance two centuries later.

The Winnats

At one time this dramatic limestone gorge west of Castleton was thought to have been caused by the roof collapse of a mighty cave system. Cave Dale, too, was thought to have originated in the same way. The favourite theory now, though, is that both limestone gorges were the result of erosion by water torrents during high rainfall periods at the end of the Ice Age.

The top of the Blue Circle cement works chimney, near Hope, can be made out above the spur on the opposite side of the gorge (top left) and the shadowy profile of Shatton Edge and Abney Moor form the main horizon four miles away beyond hidden Cave Dale and Bradwell Dale.

Across Rushup Vale

From the high road along the southern flank of Rushup Edge there's a broad vista in clear weather. The foreground farm is one of several attractive hill holdings just below the road; they can make a useful lead-in for photographs that take in the distant village of Sparrowpit strung out along the lane that climbs westwards on Peaslows Hill.

This unusual, shallow depression called Rushup Vale may not look the part but is actually the site of one of the Peak District's most dramatic happenings. Down there the streams that drain the shale grits of Rushup Edge run out onto shale and disappear from the surface down a series of swallow holes. The most dramatic of these is Giant's Hole, one of the biggest in the entire district. This is the point where the shales end and limestone comes to the surface. The water runs to great depth through faults and master joints and instead of draining, as topography would suggest, to the River Wye it surfaces a couple of miles to the east at Castleton and so runs into the Peakshole Water, Noe and Derwent. These Rushup streams actually cross a watershed by going underground.

Lamplight, Tideswell

King Edward I stayed at Tideswell in 1275 while hunting in the Royal Forest of the Peak, only a few years after it had become a separate parish. That probably propelled it to unexpected importance as a thriving market village. These flourishing times have long since passed, now it's the parish church that reminds us of such prosperity.

St. John the Baptist is one the finest three or four parish churches in Derbyshire. It is quite a rarity, too, because it was completed in one go, between 1320 and 1380. The existing chancel is one of the county's best, comparable with Norbury (see page 1).

The famous "Minstrel of the Peak", William Newton (born at Cockey Fam, Abney in 1750) is buried in the graveyard, as is Samuel Slack, considered "the most popular bass singer in England" during the last years of the eighteenth century. After retirement he came back to his roots in Tideswell and was the leading light of the village's Catch and Glee Club, which held its monthly meetings at the George Hotel (seen in this photograph), adjacent to the church which, on account of its quality and size, has come to be known as "the Cathedral of the Peak".

Long Shadows, Wardlow

A sunny summer evening near the northern edge of the White Peak. Hector Kyme set up his tripod at the roadside in Wardlow – literally "Look-out Hill" after the nearby 1,216 feet top of adjacent Wardlow Hay Cop – as the shadows lengthened. We are looking towards the north, across the stone-walled fields on Stanley Moor to the wood-crested top of Hucklow Edge. Just out of sight beyond the skyline trees is Camphill Farm, headquarters of the Derbyshire and Lancashire Gliding Club. Its name refers to the Iron Age "camp" or ramparted enclosure now forming part of the gliding airfield.

Muscovy Trio

Look over any farmyard wall in Peak hill country and you're likely to see something interesting. Some relic of bygone husbandry or throbbing life continuing; Hector Kyme was quick to spy out such gems. Here's a little family of Muscovy ducklings in a paddock at Wardlow, waiting for mother to come and cover them for the night with her own down duvet.

Wardlow Smallholding

Typical of scores of little farms on the limestone plateau this one stands beside the road at Wardlow. It has the mandatory accessory of a shelter belt – very useful in breaking the prevailing wind in the district described by Daniel Defoe as a "blasted wilderness".

White Shorthorn

Shorthorns come in a variety of colours – red, red and white, roan, dark roan, red roan, light roan, or white. Here is a white Dairy Shorthorn in a field near Great Hucklow, in the shadow of Hucklow Edge. From being the commonest dairy animal between the wars the breed is now almost a rare breed, ousted by the ubiquitous British Friesian and Holstein Friesian. Hector Kyme was always at pains to make sure animals stood out in contrast to their background. This study illustrates the point particularly well.

Hucklow Edge from Bretton

The Sheffield – Buxton turnpike came straight up from the Derwent crossing at Grindleford, a long, steep ascent to the 1,407 feet summit of Sir William Hill (named after Sir William Bagshawe after the enabling 1757 Road Act). The road heads due west from that high point, along the crest of Eyam Edge, through Bretton and on to Hucklow Edge before dropping to Great Hucklow village.

Taken on a sunny March day in 1975 this photograph shows the Barrel Inn beside the road at Bretton. The turnpike curves away to the wood on Hucklow Edge, in the foreground Rhode Island Reds seek out wall-side morsels on one of the first warm days of spring in a place J.B. Firth described as shivering "with the cold" when "winter winds are blowing". This fairly level stretch of road was once used for foot races between local athletes "for the settling of local wagers on points of speed". The only races on this highway nowadays are the speeding motorists with no interest in the broad views, or the welfare of free range poultry that they often put to flight.

Limestone Birds

A trio of Embden geese caught (after a long wait) against a dark background to accentuate their pale plumage. "White animals are the most difficult to photograph satisfactorily", Hector Kyme maintained. "Not only careful exposure, also precise printing is necessary if a blank white cut-out appearance is to be avoided"

The Eastern Fringe

Sunset, Ramsley Moor

Close beside the highest part of Fox Lane, between Cordwell Valley and Baslow, stands Godfrey's Cross. This is a medieval way marker, a guide for old time travellers on Ramsley Moor. A closer look will reveal the words "Here lies Godfrey" carved on the stone shaft. They were carved by a young Fox Lane lad, Godfrey Silcock, in about 1890 – just before he emigrated to New Zealand and left his spirit on this native moor-top.

The most interesting thing about this 1965 photograph is the distant profile of Ramsley Lodge, now but a memory overlooking the Sheffield – Baslow road (see page 91).

Wadshelf from Wigley

Three miles to the south-east of Ramsley Moor stands Wadshelf village, a bleak spot at the very edge of Eastmoor. This was once "the cultivated land of Wada" divided at the Domesday Survey into North Field, Nether Field and Wheatcroft Field. By 1800 several of the original strips within the great fields had been enclosed. About 1830 the whole area was enclosed as we see it today. This photograph, taken looking south from near Wigley hamlet, shows the 1830 enclosed land with Wadshelf beyond on a summer evening.

Miniature Moke

The photographer was especially fond of this picture. Taken at Cowley Bar, Holmesfield it epitomized the innocence of young life. It had a deeper meaning, though, for Hector Kyme was born nearby and spent a happy childhood there.

Burrs Wood and Unthank

Horsleygate Lane descends the northern flank of Cordwell Valley from hilltop Homes-field on the eastern boundary of the National Park. Here, late on a midsummer evening, the photograph (taken adjacent to Horsleygate Old Hall) reveals many secret corners of the wooded spurs dropping from the Eastern Moors.

Burrs Wood occupies the middle of the picture, tree-lined Unthank Lane crosses the fields to the left. Unthank was mentioned in documents of 1286, its name originating from the Old English for land held "without consent" or a squatter's holding. Unthank Hall is just visible, long the home of the Wright family (now of Eyam Hall). Knowles Farm stands in sunlight (upper right), deriving its name from the Old English "cnoll", a knoll or hillock, and is known to have existed in the late fifteenth century.

Holmesfield Park

The wood called Holmesfield Park lies immediately north of this hilltop village, on the slope leading down to Totley Brook which once formed the boundary between Mercia and Northumbria, now the Derbyshire – South Yorkshire border. An old bridleway leads from Woodthorpe Hall to Holmesfield church – but not through this gate!

In the Oak Wood

A n early animal study, taken in the days when free range pig keeping was still a common practice; before the time when few sows feel the sun on their backs or get their snouts in the sod.

March Morning

Hector Kyme considered nest building by rooks the true herald of spring. He took lots of photographs of their treetop activities; this is one of them, taken near his home on a windy morning in early March, just before a shower cloud hid the sun.

Only Practising

Border Collies have a well developed instinct for driving flocking animals. Any young sheepdog worth its salt will, without much human encouragement, set about rounding up anything on legs which conveniently comes to hand. Poultry are a favourite subject and the photographer remembered not having to wait long before this particular Collie set about his daily routine of driving the Maran flock around the farmyard. The proud cockerel was more of a challenge but even he complied eventually.

In Monk Wood

The largest woodland of the Barlow Valley, between Chesterfield and the eastern boundary of the National Park, is called Monk Wood because this land was given to Louth Park Monastery, in Lincolnshire's high wolds, about 1140. The monks gave permission for Barlow folk to work ironstone in the wood and smelt iron in two furnaces.

The area in which Monk Wood lies used to be a surprisingly large one, quite uncrossed by a public road. The construction of the Unstone – Dronfield Bypass in the mid seventies cut it in two. Taken before that time this summer study shows a clearing with glimpses to the broad fields at Barlow Lees, with the horizon of Eastmoor behind.

Spring Vanguard

Imagine the delight the photographer had when he came across this clump of snowdrops blooming in a Monk Wood clearing one February day in the early sixties. Had some romantic planted bulbs in this secret arbor or was it the chance of accidentally dropped garden waste? Whatever the explanation the little colony was never seen in subsequent years.

Lees Common from the Galloping Close

The ancient bridleway connecting Dronfield and Barlow crosses the open fields of Barlow Lees immediately west of Monk Wood and a couple of miles east of the nearest point of the National Park boundary. On a bright June evening the view towards Dronfield includes the sunny slopes of Lees Common and the old farm there which was the childhood home of Sir Arthur Holleley. Born in 1872 he became principal of Pophams of Plymouth, deputy Mayor and, in 1940, President of the Drapers' Chamber of Trade. In 1960 he had Lees Common rebuilt as we see it now.

The ridge-top above the farm was covered with heather and known to generations of Dronfield folk as "bilberry moors". In July family parties would gather the wild harvest there; now it is covered by planted trees.

Frustration

ector Kyme's "Robbie" was a highly intelligent dog but this particular manoeuvre proved beyond his powers to solve. Backwards, forwards, sideways – eventually he dropped his load and walked away with a single, loud bark!

A Big Laugh

Animal expressions were a favourite subject. Hector loved nothing better than waiting for domestic animals to strike an unusual or amusing pose. This photograph of a horse near his home started out as a standard portrait but, at the critical moment, it yawned!

In Chantrey Land

The still rural landscape that lies between Hector's former home at Dronfield, north-east Derbyshire, and Sheffield is called Chantrey Land. It contains the village of Norton, birthplace of Britain's greatest sculptor, Sir Francis Chantrey, and though now a truly integrated suburb of Sheffield has some grand country nearby. The note on the back of this photograph describes it as "the tallest tree near the Moss Valley", part of Chantrey Land; a magnificent specimen sycamore.

March Morning near Dronfield

Hector Kyme's friend Jim Smith still ploughed his arable land with Shires at Nether Birchitt Farm, (right on the South Yorkshire border) in the fifties. From the hilltop in the background there's a broad, westward view to the high moors of Totley Moss four miles away, inside the National Park's eastern boundary.

Through the Ford

The Barlow Brook drains eastwards from its source on Ramsley Moor, just inside the National Park's eastern boundary. It flows for six miles to join the Drone at Sheepbridge; it's also one of those confusing streams with different names along different stretches – Millthorpe Brook, Dunston Brook and Barlow Brook.

Here, just downstream of Cordwell Bridge (where it flows out of the National Park), is the ancient ford at Millthorpe. Wendy Bell's horse is enjoying this paddle in the mid-sixties. In the background (right) are the remains of Millthorpe's old corn mill, the subject soon afterwards of a disgraceful planning bungle. There had been a mill here beside the Millthorpe Brook since medieval times. The Buntings were millers here in the middle of the last century, followed by George Key, then the Haslams. The poor condition of the mill dam and increasing use of hammer mills on individual farms spelt the demise of this mill; by 1960 a builder had purchased the buildings but it was accorded Listed status to protect it. Neglect set in, the roof was removed and sold, the local authority took no action; the ruin was demolished in 1971 and an inappropriate modern dwelling now stands on its site.

Autumn in Cordwell

Cordwell Valley was a traditional beauty spot for generations of Sheffield and Chesterfield families. Well into this century, horse-drawn (later motor) charabancs brought townsfolk on summer weekends and Bank Holidays.

This was the adopted home of the pioneer socialist Edward Carpenter, who came to live at Millthorpe in 1883 and gathered round him friends and admirers that included John Galsworthy, George Bernard Shaw and H.G. Wells. Carpenter left the district in 1922 and died, aged 85, in 1929 but for years afterwards an annual pilgrimage took place in the Carpenter Field (now a cricket field) and the house he built in 1882 next to it is still known as Carpenter House, albeit much altered.

Self Portraits

Hector Kyme's clever dog "Robbie" could "count" up to ten, do many unusual tricks and obeyed commands in several languages. All this was the result of his master's patience and imagination and strangers were amazed at the rapport between dog and man. He was an inseparable companion on photographic expeditions for many years. One thing "Robbie" could not bear was thunder – summer storms reduced him to a trembling wreck long before the first peal was audible to the human ear.

Here's the pair in their Dronfield garden about 1970. Hector reassures "Robbie" as he squeezes the camera shutter's remote control bulb; he entitled the print "I'm not sure of this!"

Sundown at the Crow Stones

A commission to illustrate a new book about the Peak District in the late sixties meant that Hector was keeping an eye open for likely subjects. We had just finished an October day on the high tops when the sky bore promise of a fine sunset. Without hesitation we set out from the road-head in Derwent Dale and raced through the trees to cross the river at Slippery Stones. Trotting northwards below Swine Side we climbed steeply past the pair of shooting cabins at Bull Stones (see page 42) and on across the steep moor-slopes.

"Keep going", urged Hector as I looked back to him as he strode from tussock to tussock, keeping one eye on the gathering drama in the western sky. By the time we'd got in position at Crow Stones, not far below the lonely crest of Outer Edge, the heavens above Bleaklow were a riot of red and orange, midnight blue cloud islands punctuated the vast skyscape. A stiff wind was blowing but Hector's shouted instructions were faintly audible as I climbed onto one of the tors for this photograph.

Several photographs were taken but the first was the one eventually published and Hector was well pleased as we set off homewards through the windy dusk. It was quite dark by the time we re-crossed the packhorse bridge at Slippery Stones.

Let the photographer have the last word; it could be described as his philosophy for life. "The scenery of the high gritstone plateaux – Black Hill, Bleaklow, Kinder Scout – can be exquisite or sickeningly squalid, depending on the weather. The area is sublime for the reason of obtaining solitude (only game birds and mountain hares for companions). In these days of bulldozer and mushrooming building sites it's reassuring to know of some place that will not change from what it has been for thousands of years – and be able to escape to the fastnesses of Bleaklow for the peace of the soul".

Get more from the Peak District with . . .

TEA SHOP WALKS
IN THE PEAK DISTRICT

Our "Tea Shop Walks" feature easy walking for all the family. In this book, by Norman and June Buckley, you can walk a few miles, then reward yourself with afternoon tea, or even morning coffee, in one of the area's many and varied tea shops. The walks are planned to take in different terrains and grades of walking and a wide range of tea shops – including a farmhouse kitchen, a converted cotton mill and even the one at Chatsworth House, the area's premier stately home. £6.95 (Companion volumes for Cheshire, the Lake District, Cotswolds and other destinations are available. Ask for details!)

HALF-DAY WALKS IN THE PEAK DISTRICT
Vol 1 – The South-West

Alan Bradley's book is suitable for small children, plus adults with little time to spare, who are feeling a little older or just plain lazy! Routes are circular and details are given of points of interest, cafes, pubs and public transport. £6.95

HIGH PEAK HIKES: walking in the foothills of the Peak District

This includes a 60-mile trail passing through High Peak Borough, plus many circular walks based on the historical heritage of the area. The book is by David Frith, footpaths officer for the New Mills Group of the Ramblers Association. £6.95

PEAKLAND RIVER VALLEY WALKS

Instead of heading for the hills Tony Stephens' ambitious book explores some 200 miles of river valleys. The routes range from 8 to 33 miles and are divided into convenient sections with frequent detours to places of interest.   £7.95

More books about The Peak District

EAST CHESHIRE WALKS FROM PEAK TO PLAIN
(Third Edition): Graham Beech   £6.95

BEST PUB WALKS IN THE PEAK DISTRICT
(two volumes: Dark Peak & White Peak):
Les Lumsdon & Martin Smith   £6.95

TOWN & VILLAGE DISCOVERY TRAILS –
The Peak District: Norman James & Abigail Bristow   £6.95

MOSTLY DOWNHILL IN THE PEAK DISTRICT:
Clive Price   £6.95

THE BOGTROTTER'S GUIDE:
Exploring & Walking the Dark Peak: Chris Holmes   £6.95

WALKING PEAKLAND TRACKWAYS:
Mike Cresswell   £7.95

Sigma Leisure books are available from your local bookshop. In case of difficulty, or to obtain our complete catalogue, please contact: Sigma Leisure, 1 South Oak Lane, Wilmslow, Cheshire SK9 6AR. Phone: 01625-531035; Fax: 01625-536800

E-mail: sigma.press@zetnet.co.uk Catalogue on the web: http://www.sigmapress.co.uk

Cheques should be made payable to Sigma Press. ACCESS and VISA welcome.
Please add £2 p&p to all orders.